Contents

All around the world, plants grow in amazing variety. In order to grow, they need food. Green leaves are the food factories of each plant. Read on to discover how their shape and structure help them thrive in different environments.

Deep in a wood, many plants are growing. Beech trees stretch up towards the sunshine. Ferns unfurl their feathery fronds and carpet moss clings to the tree roots. Wood anemones spread out across the ground.

This is a living wood. All the leaves are green.

A green leaf is a food factory. It needs light from the sun, water from the soil and carbon dioxide from the air to make sugary food for the plant.

LIVING
LEAF

Judith Heneghan and **Diego Moscato**

Published in paperback in 2018 by Wayland
Copyright © Hodder and Stoughton, 2015

Editor: Nicola Edwards
Design: Anthony Hannant, Little Red Ant

ISBN 978 1 5263 0723 1
Library e-book ISBN: 978 0 7502 8766 1

Printed in China

Wayland, an imprint of
Hachette Children's Group
Part of Hodder and Stoughton
Carmelite House
50 Victoria Embankment
London EC4Y 0DZ

An Hachette UK Company
www.hachette.co.uk
www.hachettechildrens.co.uk

FSC
www.fsc.org
MIX
Paper from
responsible sources
FSC® C104740

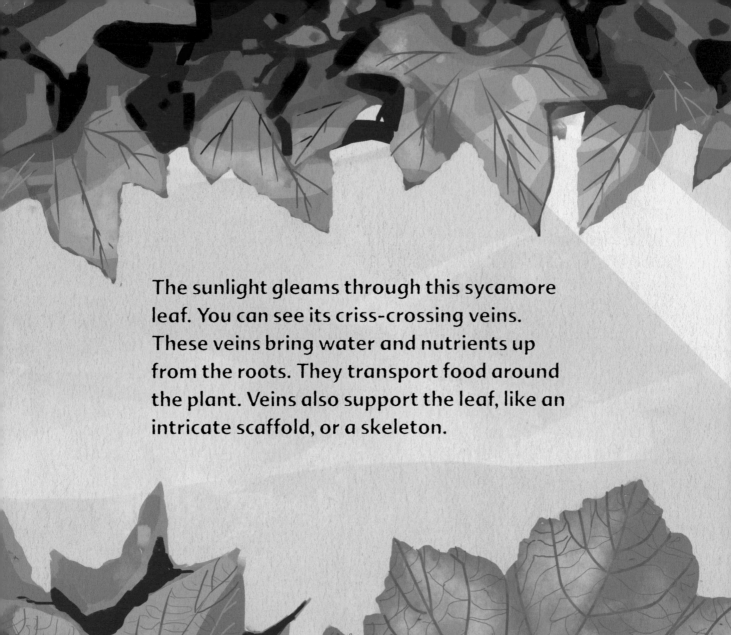

The sunlight gleams through this sycamore
leaf. You can see its criss-crossing veins.
These veins bring water and nutrients up
from the roots. They transport food around
the plant. Veins also support the leaf, like an
intricate scaffold, or a skeleton.

Each leaf is covered with tiny holes to let air in and out. Most of these holes are on the underside of the leaf. They are too tiny to see without the help of a microscope.

A dandelion grows on a patch of waste ground. A willow herb grows beside a wall. The leaves sprout at different angles so that each leaf can find the sunlight. If the light comes from one side only, leaves will bend and grow towards it.

Some plants have leaves that grow in spirals around the stem. Other plants have leaves that grow in opposite or alternate pairs. This prevents a leaf from shading the leaves below.

Leaves come in all shapes and sizes. Many are broad and flat. Others are spiky or thin. Leaves may be smooth, ridged or covered in fine hairs. A few, like the leaves of this elephant ear plant, grow as wide as your arm span.

The elephant ear plant grows in damp, shady places. Its broad leaves have a large surface area – perfect for absorbing as much sunlight as possible.

Other leaves are small, lacy, delicate as a snowflake.

The California poppy grows in dry, warm places. Its leaves are feathery, with a small surface area. A small surface area means less water is lost from the leaves during dry, hot weather.

13

Some leaves lose their green colour in the autumn. As the weather grows colder they turn deep red and gold. Then they fall to the ground.

14

Plants with leaves that fall off in the winter are called deciduous. The plant isn't dead, but it stops making food for a few months. It is waiting for spring.

As the weather gets warmer, leaf buds develop and new leaves grow.

15

Other plants are not deciduous. They keep their leaves all year round. Think of dark waxy yew, prickly holly or the spiky needles of a pine tree. We call these plants evergreen.

The leaves of this evergreen Scots Pine grow as needles, or spines. They are tough enough to survive a freezing northern winter.

Plants need water, and take it in through their roots. But they also lose water through their leaves. So how can a plant survive on a coastal sand dune? Sand drains rainwater away from the roots while the strong winds make everything dry.

in these conditions, marram grass has adapted to survive. Its narrow leaves curl inwards to reduce water loss. The hairs on the inside surface also help by trapping moisture.

19

Deserts are the hottest, driest places on Earth. Thin, delicate leaves would quickly shrivel and die here. So some plants, like this desert agave, have thick, fibrous leaves that store extra water. Their grey-green colour also helps them keep cool.

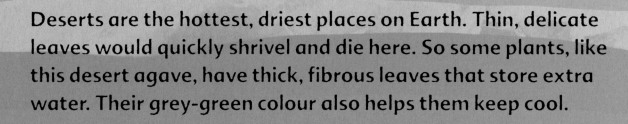

This barrel cactus has spikes instead of leaves. The spikes help to keep the plant cool by shading the bulging stem. The stem is adapted to store water and make food for the plant.

There's no shortage of water in a
tropical forest. Rain falls nearly every day.
But a water-soaked leaf attracts harmful bacteria.
The fan palm leaf above is split into segments. The wind
can blow through it and water can't pool on its surface.

Many rainforest leaves have a tip
that points downwards. These are
often called drip tips, because they
help the water drip away.

Other plants have adapted to life in the water. The huge leaves of these Amazon water lilies float on a lake in Brazil. Their surface is waxy to help keep them dry, while their underside is ridged with sturdy veins. These veins trap pockets of air which stop the leaves from sinking.

The leaves of the Amazon water lily
can grow up to two metres wide.

Leaves are full of nutrients. Animals depend on them for food. So some leaves have adapted to stay safe from predators such as insects or cattle. Prickles, stings and poisonous leaves help keep nibblers away.

These common nettles are tipped with tiny hollow hairs that pierce the skin and inject a stinging chemical.

Ragwort tastes bitter, and is poisonous for horses.

Many animals graze on meadow grass, which survives by growing from the bottom of the leaf, instead of the tip.

Leaves are amazing. They have adapted to their environment in so many ways.

Without leaves, we wouldn't survive.

We all need leaves.

When a leaf takes in carbon dioxide from the air, it releases vital oxygen back into the air. This is the oxygen we breathe.

Things to do

Green leaves are fun to grow and good to eat.

Scatter lettuce seeds or cress seeds on some moistened soil in a pot and leave them on the kitchen windowsill. If the seeds have enough water, warm air and plenty of sunlight, they will soon grow into tasty leaves.

If you find the young leaf shoots are leaning towards the sunlight, turn the pot around. In just a few hours they will lean the other way!

Glossary

adapted — developed special features in order to survive and thrive

carbon dioxide — a gas in the air used by green leaves to make food

deciduous — a plant that loses its leaves in winter

environment — the place where a plant or an animal lives

evergreen — a plant that keeps its leaves all year round

nutrients — substances a plant or animal needs for growth

oxygen — a gas released into the air by green plants

predators — animals that eat other living things

veins — hollow tubes that carry water and nutrients around the leaf

Further information

The world is full of incredible plants that have adapted to their environments in strange and wonderful ways. Here are three plants with highly unusual leaves. See what you can discover about their extraordinary adaptations.

- The Welwitchsia plant
- Lithops (often known as the stone plant)
- The pitcher plant

Index